About the Author

Jessy Harlowe is a proud born and raised Texan; she lives there now with her husband and their cats. She is currently a fifth grade English teacher, but she has dreamed of becoming an author since she was old enough to hold a pencil. All poems in this volume come from completely true events in her life. This is her first published work.

Texts I Deleted B4 Sending

Jessy Harlowe

Texts I Deleted B4 Sending

Olympia Publishers
London

www.olympiapublishers.com
OLYMPIA PAPERBACK EDITION

Copyright © Jessy Harlowe 2024

The right of Jessy Harlowe to be identified as author of
this work has been asserted in accordance with sections 77 and 78 of
the Copyright, Designs and Patents Act 1988.

All Rights Reserved

No reproduction, copy or transmission of this publication
may be made without written permission.
No paragraph of this publication may be reproduced,
copied or transmitted save with the written permission of the publisher,
or in accordance with the provisions
of the Copyright Act 1956 (as amended).

Any person who commits any unauthorized act in relation to
this publication may be liable to criminal
prosecution and civil claims for damage.

A CIP catalogue record for this title is
available from the British Library.

ISBN: 978-1-80439-277-5

This is a work of creative nonfiction. The events are portrayed to the best of the author's memory. While all the stories in this book are true, some names and identifying details have been changed to protect the privacy of the people involved.

First Published in 2024

Olympia Publishers
Tallis House
2 Tallis Street
London
EC4Y 0AB

Printed in Great Britain

Dedication

To my wonderful family: Thank you for supporting me in whatever I do. To my friends and my love: Thank you for helping me find my voice. I love you all more than words.

Acknowledgements

Thank you to my loving, supportive family; you've always been my biggest cheerleaders and support system, and I am so grateful for each and every one of you. Thank you to the love of my life; you've been with me every step of the way, and I am forever grateful that you're in my world. Thank you to my chosen family, my sweet friends; I'm so grateful that you took the time to read my words and helped me share them with the world, I adore you all. Lastly, thank you to the subjects of these stories; if you don't know who you are, that's perfectly fine with me, but if you do, please do NOT contact me. I wrote about you without using your names for a reason.

Before Reading

Before you read this,
Please keep in mind
That you will be diving
Into my subconscious,
And it's not always a fun place.
There are a lot of dark corners
That shouldn't be explored,
But getting all of this out
Has been incredibly cathartic,
And I think it may help
Someone in the future.

Consider this your content warning
For molestation,
Domestic abuse,
Social slander,
And self-harm.
If you feel triggered in any way,
Feel free to put my words down
And walk away for a while.
I understand that
My words may be painful to read,
So keep your well-being in mind.

All of these poems
Are based on true events
In my own life.
All experiences are my own,
But I want to reassure you
I am okay.
I have faced my adversity
With a brave face,
And I am stronger for it.

If you feel that you relate
To some of the more serious matters,
Please contact someone
That can help,
Or someone close to you.
You are not alone,
And you are loved
More than you know.

We are all worth it.

(symptoms)

Numbness, indifference,
Stomach roiling with nausea
With old thoughts of you.

Rosebud

The memories I have
Come in flashes of senses:
I see a yellow paisley bedspread
I hear your footsteps coming closer
I feel crippling fear that freezes me in place
I smell danger on the horizon
I taste bile rising in my throat
But then again, I was far too young
To recall much more.

In my mind,
I fabricated a story
About you doing something horrific,
But it was all a lie
To get back at you
for scaring me.
When I told my mom, though,
She knew it wasn't a lie,
And when the tests came back
With unspeakable news,
We were all torn apart.

The next thing I knew,
I was in play therapy
For a truth I didn't know.
I thought it was that same lie
Continually haunting me,
But when I tried to confess,
She gave me a sad look
And said she wished it was a lie, too.

I found out the truth
Eleven years later,
After confessing to my mom
For the millionth time
That it had all been a lie.
She finally showed me the proof,
And I was sent spiraling,
Nightmares of you
Tormenting me to this day.

I told my partner what happened,
Hoping for undying

support,
Love and sympathy.
What I got instead
Was everything I refused
To let myself think:
Words like
Dirty, ruined, broken,
Swam through my mind
Like an endless parade.

You took something
So precious
So innocent
And you sullied it,
Like crushing a rosebud
Between your fingers
Just before it was ready to bloom.
How could you?

Your one mistake
Led a happy little girl
To fear older men
For years to come,
To inherently flinch
When someone new
Tried to touch her
For the rest of her life.
You held a baby bird
Carefully in your palm,
But you laughed while
Decimating the new life
Until it was extinguished
With a whimper of fear.

I hope you regret
What you've done.
I hope you have trouble
Falling asleep,
Hazy memories circling
Through your dreams.
I hope that,
When you think back,
All those good memories
Have faded edges,
Barely resisting
Burning away
In a blaze of regret.

You single-handedly ruined me,
And I'll never know why.

(fears)

Face your fears, they said.
You will be stronger for it.
Why am I so weak?

My Life as a Canvas

I don't believe I am a person.
I believe that I am a canvas,
Freshly stretched upon its frame,
Waiting for life to color some substance.
I believe that all of my relationships,
My family, my friends, my significant others,
They all have a hand
In the art project known as me.

I came into my new life armed for success.
I was newly covered,
A brand-new canvas ready for color.
When I met you,
I hoped you would use
The bright yellows and neon greens
I had set out for the new me,
The better me that I could be.

But you didn't.
You took the beautiful brush
I had lovingly washed and dried
And you mixed all the colors on my palette together,
Creating a murky gray-brown.
That's the color you used on me,
Muddying the happy colors I had picked out
With memories of despair and discomfort.

You never tried making new colors,
Brightening my canvas with
Loyal purples or honest blues.
Instead, you highlighted your gray-brown
With more gray-brown,

Turning my beautiful canvas
To a single-noted dismal backdrop
For the dark shadows of mistreatment
To perform their acts of treachery upon.

I eventually washed your work away,
Using the tears I cried because of you
To let the paint slough off in wads,
Dripping off of me in goopy glops.
No matter how hard I scrubbed,
Or how many tears I cried,
I could never get those last remnants,
The debris left over from those dark colors,
And it still shows through to this day,
Years after we parted for good.

My canvas will never be white and clean again,
And it's all because of you.

If You Don't Know Who You Are, You're Lying

You hung over me like a shadow
From the very first moment we met.
After that first day,
Your essence pressed itself into my clothes,
My skin, my mind,
And refused to come off,
Like the wine stain from years ago
That still colors the kitchen tablecloth.

Being friends was fun
For a month,
Before you took over my life.
I never wondered
what being a Barbie doll would be like,
Not being able to choose how you look
Or how you act
Or who you interact with,
But I found out the hard way.
I sympathize with dolls so much more now.

I don't know why I let it go on for so long.
I was the frog in the pot on the stove,
Not knowing how hot the water was
Until I boiled alive.
Everyone was telling me to run,
But I refused to listen,
Even as the water scorched my skin
And threatened to overtake me.

Friendship turned to more without consent.
Suddenly, hands were moving
And innocence fell to ruin.
As spring melted winter,
So, too, did warmer days
Bring fiery arguments
And chilling confessions
That still haunt my

nightmares.

Together, we blazed like fire,
But we ended with a whimper
The day that I woke up.
I realized what I had gotten myself into,
And I chose me over you.
I cut you out like a cancer,
Because that's what you were to me:
A cancerous growth that
Refused to die naturally,
Unless I killed it myself.

Like a phoenix, I rose from the ashes
Of the singed remains of us.
I refused to continue
To let you define me,
To let you dominate me.
I chose to fight for who I wanted to be,
And I turned out better for it.

I blocked you out until you got the message,
Though sometimes, I wonder if you ever did.
If the way you continue to contact me
Is any inclination as to your true thoughts,
I don't know if you will ever get over me.
However, that is none of my concern;
I've been over you for longer than you know.

I am the best thing that ever happened to you,
But you were the worst thing to ever happen to me.

Untitled

I have never liked pain.
Growing up,
As soon as the doctor
Said the word injection,
I would throw a fit,
Screaming and crying
In fear of the needle.
In all transparency,
That anxiety lasted until adulthood,
Transitioning from loud outbursts
To quiet panic attacks,
Frantically trying to
Keep that inner five-year-old at bay.

I never thought I would hurt myself.
Then again, though,
I never thought
You could make me feel so low.
My emotions had sunk
To the bottom of the sea,
Scraping along the ocean floor
With sickening crunches.

In that moment,
I wanted to escape
The emotional turmoil
Threatening to drown me.
In that moment,
I would have done anything
To distract me from the
Tsunami of torment.

I was never very brave.
Knives and razors
Have always scared me,
So I turned away from those.
My tools were my fingernails,
Digging into my wrist
Until angry red marks stared back.
The sting was enough
To ease my mental anguish,
And I took a picture
To show you what you drove me to,
But you never cared, did you?

I wore long sleeves in the

spring,
Nervously pulling them
down, down,
Over the tiny slits in my
skin.
When my mom asked,
I told her I fell into a
bush,
But she never bought it,
Continually checking on
me
For no reason afterwards.

That was the first time,
But it wasn't the last.
For years later,
Whenever I felt that low
again,
I would rub my wrist with
my thumb,
Like trying to erase
A makeup smudge
From the face of my
heart.
When I rubbed hard
enough,
The friction peeled my
skin away,
And those same angry
marks
Met my eyes again,
So I'd rub harder, faster,
To make them fade.

That's why I got the
tattoo.
The semicolon butterfly
Flutters on my wrist,
The tips of the wings
Kissing my scars away.
The ink reminds me
That who I am now
Is stronger than
Who I once was.

No matter what anyone
throws at me,
I will always choose me.

Things I Never Told You

Fart jokes aren't funny.
For sure not the ones you told,
And the fact that
You kept telling the same one
Over and over
From a scene in a movie
No one cared about anymore
Made it seem like
You didn't know how to make a joke.

People gave us nicknames
From a popular TV show:
The two female characters,
The dumb Asian and the smart blonde.
People thought it was a joke, but
They weren't entirely wrong, I guess.

Your rules made no sense.
I couldn't wear makeup,
But I also couldn't wear my glasses
On days that my contacts
Refused to cooperate.
I couldn't spend time with friends,
But I had to text you back
Within five minutes,
Even if I had practice
Or was with family.

You drove my friends away.
The people I cared about
Saw what you were doing to me
And they ran,
Attempting to tell someone who could help,
Someone who could reach me,
But I was riding the horizon,
Always just out of reach.

Most people didn't like you.
People would associate me with you,
So they didn't talk to me.
The people who you

thought did
Said the worst things
When you weren't around.
I heard them all.

Days you weren't around
were a relief.
It was nice, not having
you in my ear,
But I still had you on my
mind,
Your incessant texts flying
in,
Despite my not being able
to check,
So then I was in trouble
Through no fault of my
own.
Maybe it wasn't great
when you were gone,
But it was even worse
when you weren't.

I didn't ghost you by
accident.
I didn't get everything
taken away at once
Like you probably
thought I did.
I finally realized what was
happening

And how miserable it
made me,
So I let the voices around
me
Finally get through.

Seeing you again wasn't a
good thing.
I never wanted to see you
again,
Yet you showed up out of
nowhere.
I had my friend take me
away,
Told him that I didn't
want you around,
And he protected me
For as long as he could.

I don't enjoy the messages
now.
The fact that you still
think
You can have access to
me in any way
Is sickening.
All I want is you gone.

You come up in my
dreams sometimes.
Everything is fine, until

you show up
And turn everything gray,
Filling me with dread and
uneasiness.
I guess that's more of a
nightmare.

Please stop trying to
contact me.
I'm so much better
without you.

(control)

What if I lose it?
The fraying shred of control
I fight to keep hold?

Phoenix

I am a phoenix: broken, yet beautiful.
As I wonder what happened to me
And listen to my tears water the ground beneath me
While watching joy in the loves of society,
I sit craving genuine bliss, but
I am a phoenix: broken, yet beautiful.

I daily fake smiles and force laughs,
But I feel no true emotion.
Embracing the familiar loneliness,
I gnaw at the thought of my own anguish.
But though I weep for my sanity,
I am a phoenix: broken, yet beautiful.

My brokenness is no weakness;
Indeed, being broken makes me stronger.
Dreaming of a better outlook,
I strive to keep a smile on my face,
Praying that "fake it 'til you make it" works.
I am a phoenix: broken, yet beautiful.

Demons

The demons came all at once.

Everything in my life was right,
But I still felt wrong,
Like the last puzzle piece
Being from a different puzzle altogether.
Suddenly, work was impossible,
And I started falling behind.

Multiple people reached out
To me and my parents
With concern in their eyes
Making them appear almost glassy,
Threatening to spill
All the emotions within.
No matter what anyone did,
Everything still felt wrong.
My family, my friends, my boyfriend,
No one was able to reach me
In the deep, dark pit of my mind.

My therapist saw the signs quickly.
Not long into treatment,
She asked if I had ever been
Genetically tested.
I had no idea how it would
Connect back to mental health,
But the psychiatrist she sent me to
Explained everything.

In your body, there's this gene
Known as the MTHFR gene.
A normal person has two intact MTHFRs.
I have only one from my parents,
Which means (among other things)
I will be clinically

depressed
For the rest of my life.
No cure, no real treatment, nothing.

At that moment, things shifted.
I realized that the demons
Who had just showed up
And made themselves at home
In the chasm of my mind
Would never leave.
I would always hear voices
Telling me how pointless I am,
Poisoning my emotions
With claims of friends hating me,
My family seeing me as a burden,
How everyone would be better off
If I just disappeared,
Melted into nothing
Like snow on the first day of spring.

I cycled through
Medication after medication,
Trying to find something
To numb the symptoms,
But the pills had their own agendas.
The chemical cocktail in my brain
Refused to come together,
Everything separating like salad dressing.
I was happy one moment,
Then devastated the next,
Never knowing when my mood would shift.
The emotional roller coaster I lived on
Never ceased, never slowed;
It drove me to the edge more than once.

I drove many people away unintentionally.
It's hard to realize that
Anyone can empathize with
The strong emotional tornado
I was often sucked into.
Explaining everything in my mind
Often worsened my mental state,
But keeping the bottle corked
Often led to an explosion.

Stuck in such an intense
tug of war,
I was often lost,
Like having no instruction
manual
When assembling
furniture.
If it's not done well
enough, it falls apart,

And you're left on the
ground,
Scratching your head
And wondering what
went wrong.

The demons are still here,
Lounging around in my
brain
Like kids sitting on
beanbags,
As comfortable as can be.
I know how to manage
them now;
Taking medication is like
Feeding the demons rich
food
That will make them less
active,

While therapy is more like
Putting on their favorite
shows
To keep them occupied
for a while.
I'm not always sure how
to manage them,
But I don't have a choice.

Managing them every day
Is a chore in itself,
But I'm determined to
keep on trying.
They only lash out
occasionally,
But when they do,
I know how to work with
it.
I take it in stride,
And I keep in mind
That demons lie, cheat,
and destroy.
Their words will not
affect me anymore.

I will scream it from
rooftops and mountains:
I am the only one that
determines my worth.

Why Anxiety Is Like an Octopus

I got to meet an octopus once.
His name was Hank,
And he was incredibly friendly.
I shook a tentacle
Like I was closing a deal.
He didn't want to let go of my hand,
Continually trying to pass it
Down his arm and to his beak.

That's how anxiety can be sometimes.
You reach into the depths,
Attempting to work together,
But it refuses to let you go.
Slowly, the tentacles move,
Shifting you closer and closer
To its gaping maw,
Hoping to swallow you whole.
Hank didn't eat my hand.

The trainer did something
To make him drop me,
And he did begrudgingly.
There's no one to help
When you're tangled in anxiety;
You have to find your own way out.

The octopus doesn't have a specific weakness,
But anxiety does:
Find the light in the darkness,
Comfort in the unknown,
And wait for the tendrils to loosen.
Even if they seem so tight
You feel as though you're about to pop,
They will loosen,
And you will be able to make it out.

Anxiety may never fully go away,
But it will retreat in the face of tranquility.

(memories)

Flashes fill my mind
Of times long past, times that once
Brought me so much joy

Too Bad You Ruined It

That night was perfect.
You picked me up from my house.
You made nice with my family.
We drove to the town square.
We wandered in and out of stores.
You bought me a stuffed penguin with lavender.
You said it would help me sleep.
We sat on a bench at the intersection.
We talked about nothing important.
You asked if you could kiss me, and I said yes.
You had never kissed anyone before me.
We kissed more in your car before night's end.
We had dinner at a fancy restaurant.
You kept staring at me.
You insisted on paying.
We drove home after seven hours together.
We didn't want to say goodnight, but we did.
You were in my dreams that night.
You were a frequent presence in them.
That night was perfect.

Popular

Ever since I was a girl,
I watched kid and teen movies
And I wished I could be popular.
I wanted to be with the queen bees,
All the girls wanting to be us, and
All the guys wanting to be with us.
I thought being popular would
Make all my dreams come true.

The year I was with you
Finally gave me a taste of popularity.
Everyone loved us, students and teachers,
They all called us the golden couple,
The champion swimmer and the cheerleader.
We were crazy about each other,
And everyone looked up to us.
We kept our friend group small,
But that made us all the closer.

The day we broke up, though,
Ripped all that popularity away.
You got your story out first,
So everyone saw me through that lens.
Suddenly, people avoided talking to me,
Preferring to talk about me instead,
Their backs turned and their voices lowered.

You ended up prom king that year,
Strolling up with one of my best friends
On each of your arms.
I felt robbed, because if we were still us,

I would have been your
queen that night,
A picture-perfect night
under the stars.

I almost wish you could
see me now,
Because, unlike you,
At least I didn't peak in
high school.

Spoiled Brat

You knew my weakness.
You knew what would send me
Spiraling back to yester-year
To the hallways of middle school
When I broke my foot
And had to use crutches
But no one offered to help with my books
So I carried them myself
But it was harder than I thought
And I tripped over nothing
Everything fell from my arms
Like they had been made of paper
I cried picking them back up
I heard in whispers around the school
That the new girl who hadn't known me
Was talking about me
Poisoning everyone against me
But she knew I couldn't refute them
Because I was too shy
They rhymed with my last name
Poked fun at my life
They were vicious like that
Like vultures circling a carcass
I barely made it out with my sanity.
If you truly loved me,
Why would you send me back there?

Wasted Energy

At this point, I don't even know if you remember me.
After all, you tossed me away so quickly,
Like I was a used tissue,
Fluttering down into the garbage.

I never thought you'd be a stranger to me.
We became friends so quickly,
And I guess we fell apart just as fast.

This year would have been ten years of being friends.
We met at a turning point for both of us,
A place to reinvent ourselves
And become whoever we wanted.
All that I wanted to become was a friend,
And you were happy to oblige.

I was there for you through everything.
I was there on picture day,
Walking in the rain
After your heart was broken.
I sent you Christmas gifts,
Things I knew would make you laugh,
And I expected nothing in return.
I gave my love freely,
And you were more than happy to take it.

When my heart was broken,
I hoped you'd return the favor,
That you'd be my shoulder to cry on
Like I was your years ago.
I wanted to stay friends,
Because we'd been friends for so long,
And I had done so much

for you.

You didn't, though, did you?
When I sent a text to our group chat
Explaining what happened,
You made fun of me,
Mocking the message
I had spent so much time on,
Wording and rewording
All the thoughts and emotions
I wanted to express.

You called me names behind my back,
Like I was someone irrelevant to you
And not the friend you shared secrets with
While listening to boy band music.
You may not know that I know,
But my real friends heard you,
And they told me the truth:

I was no longer any friend of yours,
Despite what you said to me
Away from the eyes of your spiteful friends
Who were once mine, too.

It's been years since it all happened.
I wish I could hate you,
That I could curse you and be done with it,
But I can't.
I still wish you well,
Despite the way you abandoned me
And the friendship we had.
Wherever you are,
I hope you get exactly what you deserve,
But not in a mean way,
More just whatever fate decides.

The breakup may have hurt,
But losing you is what truly broke me.

(honest)

I can't be honest.
Not really, in any case.
How could I to you?

113

I will never forget that day;
It's etched into my memory
Like a branded block of wood.
We sat down to chat like usual,
But then you said those words
That flipped my world upside down:
"So, I'm moving out."
I was sent reeling with your words,
Spiraling down an endless chasm
Of whys and how could yours.
You left me numb for days after;
It's been several years now,
And I still don't know
If I can feel anything.

The D Word

I never thought I'd hear it in this context.
I couldn't imagine the idea
Of our perfect little family
Breaking in half so suddenly,
Like a perforated chocolate bar.
I didn't expect it to happen,
To see my mom on the phone
With lawyers as she cries over paper.
I wouldn't have seen it coming,
Like a dark cloud looming
Menacingly over the horizon.
How could I have known
If I couldn't even be around for it?

Kids always think it's their fault,
Like all tension between parents
Is all because of the child.
Kids don't always understand relationships
Outside of themselves.
I never thought that necessarily,
But it was pretty telling
That you only left
Once I did.

Gray

Most people see in
Black and white,
Hot and cold,
Right and wrong.
I must be impaired, then,
Because I have never
Been able to see only one side.
People that debate with me
Are bound to get frustrated, because
I always see both sides
Coalescing in the middle,
Forming a gradient
Of shades of gray.

When everything happened,
You both promised
There wouldn't be sides,
That we could still work it out.
However, promises are like
Sand on a beach,
Easily washed away
Or taken by the tide
To settle somewhere else.

Talking to you after,
You knew I was upset,
With you and the situation,
But you stayed quiet.
You said that I had heard her side,
But not your side,
And "when I was ready"
You'd tell me your side.

It's been years now;
Will I ever hear that side?

(her)

I hope she's better,
Better at understanding
What I never could.

Losing a Friend Is Worse Than a Breakup

I actually do miss you.
Losing your friendship
Was the worst heartbreak
I've ever experienced.
Living with it,
Living with you,
Was salt in the wound.

We were so close
Almost the minute we met,
Bonding instantaneously.
We saw each other all the time,
And we told each other everything.
We made each other laugh
Harder than anyone else,
And I have so many fond memories
Now tainted because you were in them.

Remember when you asked me
If I wanted to live with you?
We were both so excited,
And we shopped for decor together
Like kids in a candy store,
Oohing and ahhing
Over every little thing.

We cried together more than once.
I remember the morning

I woke up to the sound of devastation:
Your cries shook the apartment,
And I ran to you immediately,
No bra, no glasses.
Neither of those things mattered
Because I had to get to you.

When I got to your room,
You told me of how
Your relationship had shattered,
And how your heart was in pieces.
I held you while you cried,
And I cursed the one who broke your heart,
Because whoever hurt my best friend
Would regret it forever.

The breaking of us
Was like a house blazing,
All at once
And burning everything in its path.
What should have been
A little disagreement
Turned into all-out war,
Everyone caught in the middle
Jumping to choose sides.

After we exploded,
The fire continued under the radar,
Smoldering ash masking
The live embers underneath.
We were passive aggressive

For the rest of our time together,
Leaving sticky notes on doors
And dirty dishes in the sink
In a backwards way of
Getting under the other's skin.

"Our" friends all took your side.
They didn't even bother
To let me know,
Instead making rude comments
I heard from the other side
Of my closed bedroom door.
However, my friends stayed mine,
Even the ones you thought were yours.

I still follow you on social media.
Out of curiosity,
I check from time to time.
Even though you and your newer roommate
Spread all kinds of rumors about me,
I'm glad you're doing well,
And I'm glad you seem to be happy.
Honestly and truly, I wish you the best.
Maybe that's why they call it best friends.

(feelings)

Hollow, broken, numb
Feelings I never thought would
Come with thoughts of you

10-16

i was floating by
you and your friends
i said hi after
and you hugged me
i was sitting behind
you at the game
when the halftime show
featured some movie
franchise
i had never seen
you turned in shock
offered me a loan
of DVDs I couldn't
see at the time
you messaged me later
asked if i wanted
to watch the movies
and i said yes
walking to your apartment
was terrifying at night
but you stood there
said i looked beautiful
in my yoga pants
we kept pausing it
because we'd start talking
about everything and
nothing
after the first movie
you kissed my lips
and everything had
changed.
that girl you met
then was a child,
a naive one, too,
but so were you.
why would you not
consider that a date?

Complacency

I don't know if we ever fell in love.
You may have, but looking back,
I think we more or less fell into
Complacency.

We definitely liked each other,
But honestly, I think from the start,
We would have been so much better
Staying friends.

Falling into complacency
Happened little by little over the years.
We more depended on each other
By the end.

I couldn't imagine my life without you
Mostly because I needed you there.
I needed my best friend around,
My partner in crime.

That's not to say the end didn't hurt, though.
You broke my heart when you ended it.
However, I got over you so much faster
Than I thought.

Looking back, I miss you as a friend.
I'm definitely happier now than I was then,
But I miss hanging out with you platonically,
Being complacent.

Choking

I still can't cry.
I've been sitting here for hours,
Choking on the lump of emotions
That will never release,
Like a knot stubbornly refusing to come untied.
I'm scared that,
If I try to force the emotions out,
The mangled shards of my soul
Will come out, too,
And I'll lose even more of myself.

I don't know if
Who I am now?
Is the same person
That you met so many years ago.
I don't know if
I will ever not think of you
When I think about my favorite things.
I wonder if
My favorite game
Will always be tainted
By the shadow your memory
Continues to cast,
Looming over
My favorite characters
With the ache of sentimentality.

Broken hearts can be devastating,
But honestly,
The worst part about losing you
Was losing you as a friend.
I think about our friendship a lot,
Even more now,
And I wonder if it would have survived
If we had never gotten together.
I wonder if I would still be
Who I am today?
Without the emotional roller coaster
You sent me through
During that time.

The Truth

You asked for honesty.
You never expected
The steel of your words
Is what I am using
To carve the truth
Out of my soul.

In the beginning,
I was proud of what we made.
We built a relationship
On a foundation
Of crumbling sand,
Constantly shifting
beneath our feet.
I'll never forget
The sweet burn
Of the cinnamon
You tasted of
The day everything changed.

I didn't know then,
But that was when
I became the architect
Of our demise,
When the word beloved
Would no longer describe
Me to you.

I became a stranger
Within my own mind.
I banged on the pane of glass
That existed between
My heart and my mouth,
My fists bleeding
From the shards
Of your broken heart.

The secrets inside of me
Broaden the chasm
That exists between us.
I doubt
The broken promises
We held so close
Will ever build
The future we envisioned.
I'll never forget your face
When the sunrise over the horizon
Began melting me
Like the Wicked Witch
You claimed I was.
I guess you were right
All along.

How Are You Doing?

I'm okay. Really.
I'm doing a lot better than
I thought I would.
It's been a couple months
now,
And though the first few
days
I never thought I'd
survive,
I did, and I am.

There's someone new
now.
Not a rebound
necessarily,
(That was someone else)
But something real,
Something that I think
could last,
Something arguably better
than what we had.

My new person isn't you,
But that's okay.
Through all this,
I discovered that
I never needed you,
Despite what I originally
thought.

Even though I wasn't
single for long,
It opened my eyes.
It made me realize that
I don't need a significant
other
To be happy,
To be myself.

Weirdly enough,
I think that now,
I'm more myself
Than I have been
Since before I met you.
Thank you for that.
Thank you for showing
me
That I am okay
On my own
And with someone else.

I'm okay. Really.
Not because or despite
Of anything else in my
life,
But because I'm okay
being me.
I hope you are okay being
you, too.

(friends forever)

Friends are hard to find,
Especially true-blue ones,
Especially you.

Earth, Wind, and Fire

It's harder to write to someone
That's still in my life.
That's what I'm learning from this.

If you're reading this,
I'm sure you know who you are,
And you may know what this is about.
It's nothing bad, I promise,
But I need to get this out.

We've been friends for years.
You knew me before
I became who I am now,
Before I became the "mom friend",
When I was still crazy.
We had so much fun
Every time we hung out,
And always picked up where we left off
The last time we'd seen each other.

I love that about our friendship.

We've seen each other's scars,
And we're proud of each other
For getting through them.
I remember the day
You got that bad news,
And I let you cry
As much as you needed
As we bought hair dye
And junk food together.

Boundaries have always been fluid,
But not as fluid as they became
That one visit in September.
You came out to me,
Knowing I'd been out for years,
And it got me thinking.

The term "hooking up"
Is such a broad term,

Covering everything from
a kiss
To so much more.
We didn't do much, but
I guess you could still
consider it a hookup.

You were my first positive
experience,
Especially after getting
dumped.
Afterwards, we clarified
that
Neither of us had regrets,
And we went back to
Friends as usual.

I started dating my true
love a month later,
And you started dating
someone
Not too long after that.
I guess I'm glad it
happened
While we were both
single,
If it was going to happen
at all,
But for the most part,
I'm just glad we're still
friends,
Because I love you dearly.

I'm so glad I didn't screw
anything up,
Because I'm so glad you're
still in my life.

(alcohol)

I can't have just one.
I need more, another bottle,
To escape my mind.

Sinking

I'm not blind, you know.
I see what you're doing,
And I don't recommend it.
Sometimes, talking to you
Feels like I'm in a boat
With a hole in the floor.
Sometimes, someone will stand on it,
Blocking the water from rushing in,
But they typically get bored,
And we're forced to bail out
Whatever water we can find.
I know the boat is coming down,
I know that there's nothing I can do,
But I'll stand on the hole sometimes
Just to save you.

What's the Harm?

"Come on, it'll be fun!"
She says to me,
Pulling on my arm
With that wicked grin.
She knows about my demons,
The wicked beings in my head
Pushing for more, more, more.
She's never cared,
And I love that,
So what's one night?
I take a sip, a puff, a taste,
But the next thing I know,
It's morning, she's gone,
And I'm alone with regrets.

Christmas

It was a couple days after Christmas,
And you were coming with your family
To celebrate with me and mine.
We had everything prepared:
Steaks bought, potatoes mashed,
Even games set out for after the meal.
The moment we got that call,
Everyone broke,
Like snapped rubber bands
Stretched under too much weight.
Mom cried, I screamed,
And my grandmother?
She just sat there,
Numb to the world.
We tried our hardest
To break out of our funk,
But it never truly worked.

So many things changed that night;
You were sent across the country,
And I was left not knowing anything.
I was so blindsided,
And I was mad at you
And your family
And my family
And the whole situation.
I hated that I could no longer reach you,
That you had fallen so far
Down the well with the severed rope,
Stuck at the bottom with no hope.

That night haunts me to this day,
Like a wailing ghost
Mourning for the life
It will never have again.
Does it haunt you, too?

I Hope You Know

I hope you know
How much I love you,
No matter what you do.
I hope you know
That I'm rooting for you,
Ever the cheerleader.
I hope you know
That we care about you,
All your allies behind you.
I hope you know
Who's really on your side,
Family by blood and by choice.
I hope you know
To try to stay safe,
To save you from yourself.

Can You Hear Me?

You've been so far away lately,
Literally and emotionally.
Can you even hear me?
I'm screaming for your attention,
Begging you to come back,
But I know it's pointless,
Because you can't hear me.

(anniversary)

One full year later.
I never thought this would come,
But here we are now.

Invisible

When I was a kid,
The coolest superpower
was invisibility.
I thought that,
If I practiced hard enough,
I could make myself disappear.

In middle school,
I got my wish.
Everyone looked not at me,
But through me.
No one really talked to me,
And I felt like
I could fade away
And no one would notice.

Sometimes, in large groups,
I continued using my power.
I faded into the background
Of parties, club events, dances,
Like an antisocial chameleon.
Sometimes, I would still love
To just disappear.

How dare you see me
When I'm invisible?

I Know You Know

I know you know
That when we met,
I was with someone else,
But I didn't know why.

I know you know
That our real meeting
Changed my worldview
Forever in a moment.

I know you know
That the pool party
We went to that night
Was one of my favorites.

I know you know
That our bond was instant,
And I was somehow drawn to you
Like some magnetic pull.

I know you know
That when you started playing,
My heart melted for you
Like an ice cream sandwich.

I know you know
That the first stargazing,
All I could think about
Was holding your hand.

I know you know
That our first kiss
Was an incredible memory
That I will replay forever.

I know you know
That I love you so much,
And I am so grateful
That you're in my life.

You know I know
That your last year
Had been so shaky,
You barely made it out.

You know I know
That you joining our group
Was a game changer
For everyone involved.

You know I know
That you somehow knew
I'd be important in your life,
But didn't know how yet.

You know I know
That my destroying you
Playing billiards that night
Got your mind racing.

You know I know
That when you said
You didn't need to go home yet,
It was the best decision of your life.

You know I know
That you were nervous,
Because you weren't sure
What my feelings were.

You know I know
That you never expected
Falling in love
Would be in the cards for you.

You know I know
That you love me, too
And that you'll always
See me as your angel.

Sandstone

if i was a type of rock, i think i'd be sandstone
because if you put any weight on me, i'll crumble,
fragments of my soul blowing away with the wind

maybe i was never a whole person to begin with.
maybe i was always meant to be
an amalgamation of parts,
shattered pieces fused together,
a sculpture of brokenness.

you say i can trust you,
yet when i pour out my heart,
you hold it for a second,
then replace it with your own,
expecting me to now fix you.
i come to you for comfort,
but what i get is a project,
one i don't feel prepared to complete,
but one i could never say no to.

maybe that's why confessing hurts so much.
when you hand the shards to someone else
they get cut on the sharp edges
and suddenly you're both bleeding out,
matching scars bearing matching pain,
pain you never meant to cause.

i gave you the shattered remains of me

in hopes you'd help me piece them back together,
but i was scared, so scared
that you might drop them,
and they'd shatter farther,
shards turning to slivers,
slivers turning to dust,
crunching beneath the world's feet.

these shards of broken glass,
these tendrils of sharp obscurity,
they're all i have left of who i used to be,
dropped over and over by those who came before.
is it really that much of a surprise
that i find it so hard to let go of them?

you see the cracks, but i see the light.

(thank you)

Thank you for reading.
It may not seem like much, but
I am so grateful.

To You

You are smart.
No matter what
Any number tells you,
You shine so bright.

You are valued.
You may be too close
To see your own value,
But yours is higher than you think.

You are talented.
If you compare yourself
To everyone else,
You will only find emptiness.

You are wonderful.
You may not think so,
But I'm sure I'm not
The only one to think so.

You are loved.
People might not
Always say it,
But they feel it.

In any case, I love you,
and I think the world of you.

Printed in the USA
CPSIA information can be obtained
at www.ICGtesting.com
LVHW090819170824
788329LV00001B/115